Neurocabin

Brett Stuckel

SPUYTEN DUYVIL

New York City

ISBN 978-1-969900-01-3

I

II

III

I

WISH

Cancer in a starlike cell
wiggles, chasing health,

while octopushing on the love
of dark almond chocolate,

the programmed foot
on a Hyundai's pedal,

the pillow's massage that sinks
the brain from ears and eyes

to a dream that fires
the accreted career,

fills walls with the neighbor's
clanking babybath,

issues a locker
on concrete floor.

Greed for the good is good,
said a star-stealer

poking peace into retreat,
leaving only the mission

to find it, sneak it back inside
the curling lines of lobes

before a twinkle
slithers.

CRUNCH SHOP HEALER LOG

Monday before Thanksgiving patient failed to leave work at 16:55 but stayed unpaid and closed spreadsheet at 17:25. Patient popped into boss' office for checkout but couldn't dig up name of boss' boss, showed headshaking escalating freakout like first encounter with jammed Schuylkill Expressway though by luck was not at wheel of Grand Marquis. Patient Jengaed to thin commercial carpet, froze knees, seized spit from pharynx and drooled. Boss paged get-there-fast-to-save-lives team, who rolled patient into redeye-Greyhound back-row-empty side-sleep position. Team maintained and monitored patient until box truck of saviors hauled patient to nearest crunch shop. Patient awoke perplexed fascinated while pizza-sliding out back of transport. Blinked in and out between shoot-ups of benzos and up-the-butt temp checks, gained brief focus to ask for puke bag, topped it before second sensory ambush. Treated, scanned. Big chunk of something in head. Took away license, let go with pill bottle till further fix-up.

To Be Weightless

You are born. Your weight is logged in pounds and ounces and helps doctors decide how to keep you alive. At first, weight is not a word. You cry when covered with too much cotton. Then you learn the word, and weight doesn't change. It's heavy or light, right or wrong, and you approve or you don't. If you approve, you like it, and the weight makes you happy.

You learn numbers, and weight becomes a number. It can be close, it can be far. Close to heavy, far from light, exactly thirty-four. Soon, even things you can't see have weight. Can't taste, smell, hear, touch. Abstract things—which you learn long before the word *abstract*—your joy, sadness, anger, frustration, and all of your parents' stuff they put on you. Heavy rules, light instructions, heavy spanking.

You seek heavy this, light that. Heavy on study or light on tests, heavy on helping or light on concern. You get a simple sustenance or a bunch of dollars, maybe a spouse, a family, a famous name, maybe an addiction, a record, an accident while searching for the weight you desire. Searching while loaded with the weight you already hold.

And then—*what is this?*—you're lifted by someone else. Your weight is enough for your family to bear. Your spouse dumps your Tupperware of puke—*so that's what "in sickness" means.* Doctors and nurses, only three days in and already a dozen. They walk, wheel, scan, shoot, drain, scoop, staple you—they carry you.

Now you only hold what you see and hear, smell and taste, and feel. You say, *thank you, how can I help*, you worry your weight will become more than anyone can heft. You try each day, and you wait.

Days

Brain surgery was not on New Year's Eve.

It was on the morning of the eve of New Year's Eve.

The eve of New Year's Eve was ICU.

Midnight before New Year's Eve was a swinging transfer to a rolling bed for a trip
to MRI.

But there was no MRI, only vomit in a bag.

The morning of New Year's Eve traded morphine for a cup of pudding and sleep.

Noon on New Year's Eve was MRI, no vomit.

Afternoon tea on New Year's Eve was removal of the catheter, and shyness, and the
nurse agreeing to wait in the hall, and finally painful drips.

Sunset was a transfer from ICU to a less-I room with a view of approaching dark.

New Year's Eve was reggae radio.

It was calling a water bottle a Volkswagen.

It was a fuzzy skyline, no glasses, asleep at 10 p.m. and awake at 2 a.m.,

and I had already woken after awake craniotomy,

celebrated while rolling to ICU without cheers, without a toast,

but with a new second and another and another,

and now a new New Year's Day.

HARD PART

pendulum curls on the right
because the doctor said a barber
would loosen the molded mask
around my skull, un-aiming shots
of protons into languageville left

where strands fled and fell where skin
hit velvet cake red soft as frosting
where twice-a-day moisture
staves off a dry that splits in flakes
and cuts to underground blood,

a mask too tight for a beard, bolted
to the table so protons racing
cyclotron laps into
airless tubes into
the room into
the nozzle
can scissor the trimmer of days

Under Cover

After losing half a head of hair, I grew mine back, seeking to raise my grandfather from the grave. I wanted a Calabrian grease curl waterfall. I got the too-equal bouffant of my towel-on-shoulders kitchen trims, but at least only hair was growing back. I grew a helmet to reduce the risk of an ice-slip re-opening my skull. I wanted to do something I hadn't done since age eighteen, when I grew curls inspired by Twisted Sister. And I blamed the convenient pandemic barber suppression as the reason I kept my bad hair secrets between cut suggestions and whyquestions and gel-combed sessions on Zoom to let myself avoid killing my hair too soon.

Oyster Hunter

Swallow chemicals,
compressed or sealed
into shells, unsure

of what your gut
will dredge.

Kick down
a pint of water.

Hope the flood
dams the pills
and breaks them
and they glide

through blood, plunge
into brain, sink
molecules spotted
by the medic

too big to
dive inside.

And a Towel Between Me and the Sheets

The boxer briefs
I used to wear
for dates,
I wear tonight,
an almost-diaper,
toilet paper
stuffed in back,
an ass-pad,
because my stomach
that used to wake
me up each hour
cannot contend
with sleep
so deep that sleeping
makes me tired.

Sound Effects

A sky turned white
by stretched gauze
above parallel mountains

where muted leaves
remind me
of north-frost

shingles creaking over
sidewalk in the budding
cold of fall's arrival

is the almost-silence of snow.

Play Time

Give a cat something to hunt—
nothing alive by luck
but a squeezeball, kick-roll it
toward the base of the scratchpost tower
where she sleeps on folded old towels of peace,
maybe squeak a hint pan-species from your lips
and teeth and still-drawn breath,
wake the silent stalker of our worries,
pray as she descends without
the diagnosis keeping us awake
and claws the whirling doubt we stumble on
and rocks from side to side atop her back,
no scar or tingle, no chemo skin
or cells or radiation aches,
only fangs sunk into cotton,
the cuts we need to make.

LATE REFLECTION

I was told to do sit-ups
to strengthen my core
against bodily injury,
to prolong my life,

And so I tucked ankles
under the anchor
of the padded bench
and crossed my arms
over my chest
and sat up.

A desire arrived
to check my progress,
to inspect my body
for ridges of vigor.

I lifted my shirt
for the wall.
Muscles leaned on
skin, exhausted:
a change, but small.

My surprise was not
the mirror's fault—
it shows who's
here, not
who is not.

38, No Coffee

Ginger tea sipped
to steady the stomach,
dipped in hot water

in a porcelain mug
bearing the seal of where
I went to school,

when I thought
I wouldn't drink tea
without five boozes

till I was old and retired
in sun with ice and lemon.
But tea is for any age

like death   so steep
and sip and steady
and wait.

II

33 Sessions

I walk Philadelphia sidewalks masked and walk faster or slower or stop to not pass
other people, to walk west and cross Walnut Street Bridge

to medicine, centered, advancing billions, sneak to the basement, open
doors with a square of paper towel to check in with a nurse, who, masked,

slides a thermometer under my tongue, probes and searches until a push
on the third try beeps, to pace the waiting hall beside the waiting

room, pace along photos of Iceland, Kyoto, Bondi Beach, and travel
ways from where I stand and smear a blue plastic pager wet with Purel,

though they always have and always will wipe it with bleach from one
page to the next, and when it carnivals five orange bulbs, walk

to the dressing rooms, try for the room that has been dressed in least often
and pack my jacket and vest and button-down and t-shirt

and pants and leather belt in a garbage-bag fort against a locker,
the left-behind of whoever locked it last, and don a HUP gown pulled

from the wooden cabinet where gowns are stacked, after guessing which gown
was coughed on, squeezed, breathed on least often, and wait in the back

of the waitroom, chairs in a *U* for a flatscreen of home renovation in Texas, Toronto
gardens in deep Mississippi, home sales along freight tracks,

and wait where there's space between others gowned, waiting for buzzes, the same
buzz I wait for, and when the pager buzzes again, I walk

to *Proton Room 1* and the trio with greetings, rest pager and key and glasses
on the wet, sterile seat of a black plastic chair,

step to the bullseye dart table, stair-climb and sit, push off my sneakers, spin,
lower my head to the cupper of foam, wiggle my buttocks

onto the folded towel the team provides with loving advice to fatten my heinie,
and they roll a soft yoga log under my angled knees,

further protecting tail nerves from pain, from pinches, from pressing
into the metal, and they put my head under the molded mask, bolt in four

bolts, two on each side, and snug webbing onto my face to keep my jaw tight,
and hand me left-right handles of ropes to pull

a board tight to my soles like I'm standing on a playground swing,
and they put half a blanket over my stomach, helping anchor all

in place, and I breathe through my nose and focus my eyes
closed, puff up my stomach on each inhalation, snorkel dive the Barrier Reef,

ignore the stereo's *Cat's in the Cradle* while the team rotates housing
that circles the table to position a nozzle beside me to shoot protons

brain tailored by blades while I talked of Granada, brain foamy
om breakfast capsules of chemo, to shoot protons in but not out as

ie at the center of analog hands, while the nozzle rounds
r readings in languageville left. The team's talk fades, they leave the room,

id I wait, alone, for the zap of protons, and I see blue laser spaghetti,
ie stitch changes with every shot, and I smell it

issing through plastic, the mask, pulling the horn of the nose in wet-knotted brain,
see avalanche rainbows rise from the floor of my eyelids

a green-lit prohibited room, or see nothing at all, nor smell, nor hear
or touch nor taste, and the team comes back and clanks

id bangs and rotates and locks and twists the table I'm bound to, leaves
ain, and I wait for snow—and return with *you can*

op those handles, you're done, and unbolt the mask molded for my Calabrian nose,
ore the mask somewhere for twenty-four hours, and I drop handles,

ise knees, and they pull out the lifter, toss blankets to laundry, and I roll
pardon my tailbone and keep my eyes closed until

ie table returns to zero position and red laser flashes over the lid
f the left-side eye as I align with center and sit up

id re-tie the neck of my gown, with the toes of a foot lift a sneaker,
ull it on without worries of a careless reveal,

other foot next, step down from the table, thank the team
and thank them again, *hope to see you tomorrow,* grab my pager and key,

put on the glasses, walk back and change, nod through the crowd seated
waiting to wait, drop the pager for wipe-down, go in a toilet,

wash hands, dry, retie the bandana to guard the baldness, walk upstairs, evading
breaths, up two to 1, down one to G, stalk the ten-foot-

wide spinning front door, when it's empty, hop in, stride out, pass
the duo checking arrivals, *right behind you,* walk southwest for a route northeast,

around the purring parking garage, walk six feet from heading-home
doctors and patients and nurses and helpers, walk six feet from today to the next.

III

First Handwritten Note After Awake Craniotomy

Nice to be making a note for the new decate! Eating oatmeal and peanut butter and rainsen—oh my! Yesterday made the move from the hospital back to our house (recall, approvement). Took a shower for the first time yesterday, with baby shampoo for the head, very light, trying to wash our...oh Jesus, how many metal seriads? 40? Something like that. Just about everything we do needs to be done clerfiyd, done right just to do the item—brush teeth, wearing clothes, putting food in place, sitting, not putting things too low, riding stories...Will be a lot more stiff, a lot more safure—more safe when we can get the medal chips out of my head. Just don't want to bent it too much. Little by little, making head feel better, even the right side of the head feels just a bit...off!...getting there.

Less

Raised in find-something-to-worry-about Westchester, where despite the acre and Grand Caravan and reservoir trails, everything was about to go wrong, and everyone was Wall Street-competing to find each other's flaws and short sell. But the worries weren't enough to make me more than quirky until cancer rang the skull-market bell and my leveraged portfolio sank, until the pandemic matched my sabotage with mosquito swarms that grew into bees into crows into choppers into B-2 bombers. I chased a job of demotion, boring, passing handoffs from home, alone with a laptop, a few clicks a day. I did not trust time, myself, people, or physics, so the planned relaxation of a pre-scan trip to Seneca Lake became a worry-tour of the cleanliness of a paper napkin, the diner-table neighbors, the car stopped and waving to let us cross.

To the Medical Student

I wish I wasn't trying to impress you as a patient who has so much to teach about what we think when we think about cancer. I wish I wasn't trying to impress my friends, my family, to appear as someone worth eighty years of love halved doubled-up into forty. I wish I wasn't trying to impress myself as someone who achieved the death that cancer challenged them to find. I wish I had always thought I was worthy of an attention constellation, of intelligent love, and my own satisfaction with what I have and what I've found and how I must orbit, change seasons, and grow. I wish this had reached my thoughts while staring at a star that's not anaplastic astrocytoma.

Normal Operation

Don't tell me I can't
[use my brain to] build
with words that revive
your brain and make
you proud to share
a post with a link to a page
containing the words,
distributing words,
holding the words,
spreading to others,
here by post or not,
who, after finding
and counting the words,
make what they feel
while riding a tickle
of brain stimulation
and power words to build
their brain to a tower
bigger than mine, wider,
fatter, stronger, more secure,
cozier, safer, snugglier too,
for which if I knew
I'd supplied raw gear,
I'd breathe and tell you
I use and can use [my] brain.

Hip Old Campus

To be a psychology major
with a brain tumor detected
fifteen years after graduation
in the left temporal lobe
is to have memory
with memories of memory
welcomed home
when I am told
how memory struggles.

MAGNETS

The first touch is in the MRI locker room, my clothes and ring off, disposable underpants on. Then the gown, then the rubber-soled socks that tomorrow will touch a person's life. Then, the vein touched with a needle to make a tunnel for cold contrast.

Then the flat sliding plank, the cylinder under my knees, the thin blanket up to the waist. Then the earplugs. I lie back with my head on the cup. I ask for tight supports to hold my skull. They coil the IV tube around my thumb to make sure I don't knock over the scan. They give me a squeezeball to tell them if I need help.

And then they slide me in, almost touch the circular walls of magnetic resonance. The clicks and bass and beat and thrum punch through my earplugs. I don't mind. They are probing now by hand. With each boom, they have something to learn from, to help me know what comes next.

Three hours later, I'm changed and waiting with my wife in the cancer center. Room 12 or 15 or 18. The doctor knocks. Their tone says more than the screen. They listen, feel our worries, and with only words and questions, careful eyes and nods, see what the machine cannot. We feel their support on the bumpy turnpike home, and each day for eight weeks until we return.

Supply Chain

Surgery and radiation and chemo changed my route. Sank proper nouns. Made me invent short word hops between islands. But what if the words are only stowed by my pills? Twice a day, an anti-seizure boat sails to my belly. Does it containerize words? I don't dare stop the trade to find out.

To the Sender of the Letter to the Editor

You asked me to imagine the future
and all I can say is cliché
for the youth bubbles
who think they'll be a grandparent

for the cancer-grammers
who balk at your assumption
for the workplace roar coach on the go-go-go
for the star-staring beach bumbler

versed in the Zodiac
but still I try to imagine the future
with cash at the perfect percentage
and a ranch house where mountain meets

water that won't flood
and oatmeal soupy yet igniting each morning
and our couch-loving kitten
also grown without babies

on the porch off the road
letting others imagine
and neither tell us
nor distract us from today.

I'VE BEEN TOLD TO TAKE NAPS

On a really good night, when I close my eyes and see a flash in the upper right corner, I don't worry that it's the splash I saw last year until steroids and time shrunk my brain back to a size more friendly to eyes. I hope I can keep bedtime hallucinations without the mushroomcap tumor they came from. If the worry peeks in, I remind myself that these are just bedtime sights I've learned to see, rooted in a new fake candle out the window in the yoga teacher's backyard.

And on a really bad night, I forget that a bad night can be refined by moving to the couch with the yawning, slow-blinking cat and reading a magazine as a dream, where real estate ads are curiosities and not one of the many dollar-sign shoulds I throw in the cart while looping, aisle by aisle, around the grocery I can't escape on a really bad night.

Every Hour / Datamonster

Data says my frequency of data collection has been reduced, but still, I must apply what I know of data to learn more about data, to know enough to teach what data says to those who don't speak data, an exchange that will improve my data at the bank, if not my body, until trend replaces trend, and I become historic.

I AM PROCESSABLE

I still imagine sixty-five but feel lucky for forty on day twenty-four in two months.

But not more than half the days have been spent, summed, lived, cashed out on twenty-four hours of zero treatment. The twenty-twenty-one spiral agenda book in drawer two of five of the steel file cabinet says the last milligrams of temozolomide went down Friday

four/nine/twenty-one when I was six-point-eight pounds below five/twenty-three/twenty-two and couldn't curl a twenty-five pound barbell without worry of tears.

The last three pills to sum to one dose went down five-hundred and one days after one seizure that called one ambulance nine-one-zero days before today, today one-hundred-eighty-five before one-thousand-ninety-five, which is three of three to five years.

Ninety-two days from today is eight/twenty-four/twenty-two, one month of thirty-one days after my fortieth year, my four-hundred-eighty-first month, my

fourteen-thousand-six-hundred-and-first day, which is more than most of the one-hundred-seventeen billion humans who lived and live on a space rock filled with big numbers.

Who Cares

I'm scared I care more about success than life. Scared that since I said I have cancer, I must prove it by disappearing. But have I ever cared about success? I drove a 1996 Mercury Grand Marquis for the past eight years and only sold it when seizures stole my license. After graduation, who expects Utica to Granada to Santiago de Compostela to Chicago to Norwich to Goa to Annapurna? En route or not, busses break down. The way to care is not caring. Why beat up the bus, why curse the driver, why imagine competition between death and survival?

The Predator

To fall asleep fast as a cat—
I'll keep that new habit I have
until I cuddle up
on the kitchen sink's comfy
feet mat before the last
nap of this snapped-back-together
brain-heart-intestines stack,
in which case I'll prowl
and scratch the couch
and beg for another snack.

I Am Lucky

I am a fat feaster on the chart slice of happiness
that I made grow from the skinny me-pie
that left me prowling for leftovers
in the Old Stone Jug knowing I saved
with a pitcher to use as my mug,
in Tom Cavallo's pasta pot at 1:30 a.m.
stomping and singing to Journey.
It's OK [you] always thought happiness was
a dollar-store Tastykake on sale
because its expiration date is next week,
[Seinfeld and Friends and Frasier]
and it's OK you scoff at the laugh track
before accepting the need to clean out
the head is something everyone has.

IV

Each Time I Dig I Get Used to the Dark

when I can't remember the word

brrrr

I no longer tell myself words

eye

that punish for the loss

at

of the chunk that held the word,

whir

now I roll words in the left

ol'

frontal cave that amaze the same as

maze / may / May

a tour of shades below the grass

tore / torn

where stalagmites and stalactites bite

act

and find words though not

fine

gold are still worthy

ill

and bring them to the surface

inn

encouraged by the something

err

found to make the search worthwhile.

The Freezer Is the Microwave

I don't know if I'm different
because of damage to brain cells,
added-up hours of worry,
digestive stress from the lockdown of anti-nausea pills,
or shocking bills somehow shockingly paid,
because now I talk at work in cliches
because I have bigger fish to fry.

I don't know if I'm different
than I would have been at forty and four months
if thirty-seven and six months hadn't gifted
eighteen months of treatment
and ongoing three-month scans,
like the scan in three days
that might be different,
or might not be
different, leaving me
different
the same
for another three months.

CATALOGUE

I need a gray wool hat
to hide the question-mark
scar that curves around
my words and drops
below my sideburn.

I like every person
smiling at me
and the world I forget
to smile at,
and I like their promise

of thirty percent
off because I want
every bit possible off
the shelves and balance
sheets of the skull.

I want to worry
about clothing and whether
to buy shirts designed
to be worn untucked
or not, to return

to worries that stem
from how to spend
and when to wear
new hats and not what's
growing underneath.

PREDICTABLE UNPREDICTABLE OUTPUT

I want to absorb the energy
that powers the magnets
of tomorrow's scan.
I want science to engineer
a plank I can slide inside
a life ring and know
my engine output
for the next two months.

I want Time to rest
on its back and be still
for half an hour
with its head wedged
in place, so just for a day,
it doesn't ding us
with invisible thumps.

My wife and I stood
bedside as her father
breathed slower and stopped,
and we floated out
of the Manor Care
ground floor, room eleven
or twelve, or who knows.

I ignored my phone
for a day, the energy
of silence keeping us safe.

I will need energy
tomorrow to ride the car,
the train, the plank,
the wait, the truth of what
energy has been building.

I felt more tired on the trail
in Frenchtown
than I did the next day
when her father went down.

THIS PAST WEEKEND WHILE ALONE IN OUR APARTMENT

I remove the box fan from the window and lay it front-down on the hardwood floor under the skylight and unscrew six tiny Phillips heads and clink them into a white cereal bowl and remove the fan's plastic back and sit it flat on an empty cereal box

and with disinfectant wipes pull wetness along each tilted blade and collect cat hair and neighbor nighttime tobacco oil and laundry skin dust and dump the wipe and do it again with another, and then wipe the inside edges, the back of the fan's front, pull the wipe from the tip of the cord backward to its base

to not loosen the connection to the shiny penny coils of the old yet dignified induction motor, and without a compressed air spray can, break the rules and use a plastic straw to push dust from the spaces ready to grow fields of magnetism, then pick up the bits and dump them away

and stand and take off my clothes and carry the dustbound back cover into the shower with the blue-haired scrub brush designed like an iron and squat and scrub gently the old plastic, not knowing how much pressure will break the thin creakers and spin the back a quarter-turn four times

so every part gets scrubbed from every direction, then raise it and rinse it and turn off the shower and dry what I can and lift it to the living room and stand it on the carpet against the table facing the window to dry and piece it together and piece it together

and return it to the window next to her side of the bed before she gets home from the grocery and pharmacy Sunday rounds and, try as I might, fail to resist telling her I cleaned the fan while she was gone because I don't want our spinning to break.

CHECKED OUT

I imagine we will remember how to imagine the future. I imagine imagining the future will help us remember. I imagine wearing a belt from Vancouver around sandy chinos up the stairs behind you to the plane home to Vermont after our winter in Havana. I imagine next week, I'll buy the Leatherman multi-tool I promised myself last December and find enough barn junk to pry, twist, and grab that I break it and buy another. I imagine we'll drive neglected suits to Goodwill after your father fulfills his wish for discount cremation and we slide him into the seacoast miniature mausoleum between his parents. I imagine math and the world and our cells will align and we will work for free with carts of books and after we will sit on the leaning-back couch by the window over the river until the clock lifts us up from the shelf.

WHERE WE RAN FROM

We circled the trail under sun
in the month of only rain
understanding the season spring
and rolled in and out of side-legs

along the Delaware River—the hilltop,
the dock, the odd house,
the bridge, sipped coffee after noon
with face-sized cookies and trusted

the sky for the fire ahead.
We drove to a spot in the forest
and backed in and built the home
and stacked wood and burned wood

and fried sausage and onion and pepper
and the rain began, and we strung up a tarp
and sat and sipped and trusted in showers,
but the storm turned

and beat the trees into cracks,
and we lay awake captured
by thunder and snaps and olive drops of wet
landing just above our heads,

and at four-thirty, toppled all and raced
into dark, burned gas, crunched
over gravel, fought slides and parked

Grounded

I am not on shore
I will not be on shore
I am in a boat floating

off of the shore
sometimes toward shore
sometimes away

cut from the hunt-boat
I woke on one day
and thought would

carry me back to the shore
but instead it put me on
a smaller boat

to float barely
until I saw
and recalled

I had been on the
big boat sliding
along the horizon

toward which I had paddled
since being freed by the cut
but I will never reboard

only paddle-pass
and tug their eyes toward rocks
and hope they find

there is no such
thing as shore.

Blood Door

I can slip out fast
like the stool of this morning
that plopped me back to the stall at work
to compare if that shat looked like this

and ask if it paddles to the Delaware River
or loops me back to a needle of anesthesia
so I wipe and wrap
in Kleenex and put it on

the floor and wash
and go get my phone
and take a picture of scarlet whirling,
hiding underwater, a celebrity

carpet, a siren, a stoplight,
I will share this place
with the doctor and ask
where do I go next.

Spy vs. Spy

I want to be a spy. And why I say that is why I'm not a spy. I say that because I watch. I watch from the outside. Now I watch my insides from the inside. I know it is and is not in my head. I watch for the words I want to say. Sometimes I find them. Decrypt them. Use them and let them go. I know things can flip fast. Sometimes I stare too long and my watch spins and I see me watching me and I'm caught. I don't know if I can investigate radiation again. If I can go back to smuggling chemicals. If one day I won't be able to pocket the doctor's intel and sneak home on the train.

What the Guy Sitting Next to Me at the Bar Said to the Cancerous Side of My Head

Badass skull scar, big ass question mark, were you riding?
My brother went over the handlebars in Zion,
my dentist put his hand in the snowblower,
all I have is the Hot Wheels hood that sliced my falling knee.

How did they stitch it up? What—you got stapled?
Forty-six of 'em, killer, man, you got to keep those sides tight,
tell the barber you want a 1, all the way up,
a pre-emptive shutdown of road rage.

People buy you shots? They know
you're a last-call fist-launcher, want to
get in your corner,
metal plate under there? Does it keep

you awake? Did you break
the airport scanner? The TSA,
they see it and search you, or say right
this way, Afghanistan ass-kicker,

was it a Siberian gulag
inquiry table,
a year trapped on one of those
feisty islands?

Don't worry, I know
you can't tell me, I'm not
asking, I'm just,
sorry, seriously, don't

want to pry, my
bad, I'm out—
bartender, tab.

GOLD

I am dad
to my dad.
I am grandfather
to myself.
Fast old me
helps was-young me
listen, and
was-young me
helps now-old me
go easy.

Old is how old
you are divided
by how old
you'll live to be,
a denominator
changing daily,
though some think
they predict it
until both
link hands
and dance
off with new
life in their grasp.

HORIZONS

Have I already done
the last pull-up
I'll ever do
is not what
the pull-up coach
wants you to ever think,
but the bar
wonders every time
you drop down
onto woodchips
if you'll ever jump
again
and grab and rise
to pull eyes even
then see over
into the next pull.

Fall Up

Last hill up First Avenue above
the unmarked graves of revolution,
on a sidewalk broken by snow and morning sun.
I tried to go fast. I stared at my watch,

ready to quit when it beeped for mile three.
A Sunday on which I hadn't napped—
my knees dozed off: watch-watching
said we're on a couch, not in a sprint.

The outside of my left shoe smacked a tooth
of concrete, going down I palmed the rough
and rolled onto my hip, watch not cracked
but not protected; skull intact, defended.

Nobody on their porch to help.
Didn't know I ran until I fell.

V

CARRIED

a truck hauls trash
until the driver sleeps
and dies behind the wheel

turquoise and clear
approach, stop or pass
siren and ice

trash hauler follows
rolls to the shoulder
lifts, hauls us away

SEEK STRIKE DESTROY

tank skills
kill tanks
eat beans
fill pockets

roll on
roll over
dig holes
wait quiet

slip away
never here
lie, wait
lay waste

sharpen sticks
belt notches
notch belts
wind watches

watch wind
know moves
move nos
wait, slay

sleep light
light sleep
hour now:
now ours

El Camborio

I want to go home and bring you
to Granada's Albayzín,

watch the fin-snowcap
of Sierra Nevada surrounded by Moroccan tea

and blue-blast flowers and staircase
kittens with the same unknowns

and if the price to ship a body
home is too much, leave me in the

duende cave where we dance until dawn.

EXTRA TIME TOPPING

I will retire my retirement
to buy back days

and fly to Aruba
with a sunblocker hat

or just rent a barnhouse
eight miles from Kingston

where I'll turn up the heat
to warm six-thousand square feet

of eighteen-inch wood plank floors
to cozy my slippers

when I return inside
from the unshoveled deck

and snow-softened chair
after a teal-sky rise

over the Hudson
and at night tip the driver

twice the price of the pie

Rest Stop

There's a gas station off
Route 9 in Poughkeepsie
where pizza spins
and never congeals,
where you don't have any
addictions but Twizzlers.

This is where every road
ends and every road begins.
Every napkin perfectly placed,
and in back, a Comet-clean
one-seater toilet. Take as long as
you want. No one will knock.

ON THE ROAD, ABOVE

to be in Pennsylvania January sun
despite all the maps I've thrown away
and other plans I've let childhood
drop in my pocket a broken fishhook
promoted to the bottom of the lake:

cry thankful for new hopes found
CDs under the seat of a Cutlass
Cruiser wagon with a tapestry
stapled as a better headliner clean
not blocking the dome light filling
the driving parked and driving night

Snow Path

I have wandered
cold places
I do not remember
until I wander into
a place as cold
and silent as the
past I did not realize
would become
the quiet I wish
to reclaim

Brother Oat

What occurs in the mind of an oat
scooped but fallen outside the bowl
to counter to floor to dirt
after growth in the sun in a field,
after picked and grouped and tubbed,
after travel so far with so many
just to be discarded, deemed unworthy
of a finger-pinch, never dropped in the bowl
to soak and share its fat and fiber.
What occurs in the mind of an oat
left behind, alone—
none here to ask, we pick each other up.

Uplifting

The moment
before you die,
glasses materialize
on your nose:
old heavy tortoise,
lower than you've ever
worn glasses,
and you see the pyramid's
oscillating beacon
at the apex high above
the bed in which you lie,
but where you focus
your hint of smile
is the weight of the frames,
which gently close your nostrils
after your lungs are empty,
before the fingertips
close your eyes.

SOUNDTEST

When I lose
my language,
I will not know
which neighbor-wish
is keeping me awake.

I will hear them
as in baby days,
remember:
I lived then,
and I am
living now.

Followers

passed away
is more than
past, away

how far away
any can be

they are past
we are passed

and they pass
the path
to us

BEFORE THE END

Heaven is festival powder
rainbowing a train track
sliding to a station
on the banks of a river
with an arched shade roof

on Parthenon columns
over the platforms'
open-top cars
with benches and
a spot for you

The train pulls out
along the river,
and you miss it—
you're squatting in the bathroom,
feet soaked in clogwater
comfortable regardless

You soap with a streaked bar
found at the sink
which typically would
make you want to
wash your hands after
but not today

ACKNOWLEDGMENTS

Many thanks to the editors, readers, and teams who first published these poems:

Knee Brace Press: "38, No Coffee"

Libre: "The Freezer Is the Microwave"

Magnets and Ladders: "Late Reflection" and "Play Time"

Rogue Agent: "What the Guy Sitting Next to Me at the Bar Said to the Cancerous Side of My Head"

Wordgathering: "Catalogue," "Soundtest," and "Wish"

"Before the End," "Snow Path," and "Uplifting" also appear in the micro-chapbook *Outerbridge Shelter* (Ghost City Press, 2018).

"Checked Out" also appears in the micro-chapbook *Limber Days* (Ghost City Press, 2025).

"To Be Weightless" also appears in *Falling to Pieces/Staying Together*, a collection from the Penn Medicine Abramson Cancer Center's Writing a Life program.

Thank you to my fellow workers who called the ambulance, to the ambulance crew for your emergency response, and to the ER team for finding the tumor. Thank you to Penn Medicine: the University of Pennsylvania Health System and the Perelman School of Medicine, the teams of the Brain Tumor Center, the Neurosurgery Department, the Perelman Center for Advanced Medicine, the Roberts Proton Therapy Center, the Abramson Cancer Center, and the Quality of Life programs, especially Writing a Life.

Thank you to the National Brain Tumor Society and the American Brain Tumor Association for your research and advocacy. To the American Cancer Society for our residence at the Philadelphia Hope Lodge. To Triage Cancer for your legal and practical guidance. To the Cassie Hines Shoes Cancer Foundation for the adventure.

Thank you to Deborah Burnham for leading Writing a Life, and thank you to all who gather and listen and share. Thank you, Deb, for your daring prompts, your encouragement, and your prohibition of shoulds.

Thank you to Jane Huffman for helping me learn and re-learn what language can do.

Thank you to Spuyten Duyvil Publishing, Tod Thilleman, Aurelia Lavalee, and team for your fast gamble to share this work. Thank you to Charlie Baker for the cover photo and Petra Somers for the portrait.

Thank you to my friends for your motivation, tolerance, and oomph.

Thank you to my family for your optimism and support. Special thanks to my brother, Mark, for your delicate Philly driving.

And thank you most of all to my wife, Megan: Each day I am thankful for you.

Brett Stuckel is the author of chapbooks *Outerbridge Shelter* (2018) and *Limber Days* (2025) from Ghost City Press. His work has appeared in *Electric Literature*, *Wordgathering*, *Split Lip Magazine*, and elsewhere. His flash fiction was selected for the 2018 Wigleaf Top 50. He was diagnosed with Grade 3 Astrocytoma in 2020. He lives in Bethlehem, Pennsylvania, and is online at www.brettstuckel.com.

www.ingramcontent.com/pod-product-compliance
Lightning Source LLC
Chambersburg PA
CBHW020803130626
46554CB00006B/2294